Hello, Goodbye, Peace

A Play in One Act

By Gabriel Davis

gabriel@alumni.cmu.edu
gabrielbdavis.com

Cast
1 w, 1 m

Characters
Alina
Rob

Time & Setting
Present day, Manhattan. Settings are fluid throughout the play,
shifting between various locations.

(Two spot or area lights up to show Alina and Rob. Rob is
sipping a martini)

ROB

Hello.

ALINA

Goodbye!

ROB
(Holds the toothpick with olive on it out toward her)
Peace?

ALINA
(Turns away from him, arms crossed)
Men!

ROB

Women!
(Eats the olive)

ALINA

They're from Mars.

ROB

They're from Venus!
(Sips his martini)

ALINA
Think they own the world 'cause they got a penis!
(Holds her hand out for the drink)

ROB
(Handing her the glass)
This is the story of a man and a woman falling in love.

ALINA
This is the story of a woman making a terrible mistake.

(She downs the martini and hands him the empty glass)

                    ROB

Maybe he made a few misteps.

                   ALINA

He was a pompous ass!

                    ROB

He was a money guy.

                   ALINA

The end is in the beginning. He had cash and no manners.

         (Set reveals itself to be a fine American coffee chain. She is a
         barista, making his latte. He is a customer, face buried in his
         phone)

                    ROB

She had no cash and no manners.

                   ALINA

Face buried in that phone. What's so important he can't even
LOOK at the human being he's just asked to make him a latte … ?

                    ROB

He felt her watching him.   Staring. But his mind was computing,
watching stocks, tracking hundreds of moving numbers waiting,
waiting, waiting … sell.

                   ALINA

She wasn't staring.

                    ROB

She so was.

                   ALINA

She knew by the tailored suit she did not like him.

                    ROB

Oh she liked him.

                         ALINA
Don't misinterpret lust as like.   Lust is an instinct. Like is … God!
It was so annoying, he didn't look up once … I decided to just stand
there and hold onto his coffee. Maybe he'd realize I hadn't put it up
on the counter yet, that too much time had passed …but he didn't.
He just kept staring at that phone …
          (She clears her throat a few times, still nothing … she speaks
          to him)
Have you ever heard the term "Latte Factor"?
          (He looks up)

                         ROB
Excuse me?

                         ALINA
"Latte Factor." It means being destitute at retirement age because
you bought too many lattes. But I think it's not an all-inclusive
definition. Latte Factor should also refer to the factor of humanity
that is lost in the ordering of the lattes. Do you know what I mean?

                         ROB
I know I'd like a latte …

                         ALINA
And I'd like to change the world! I'd like all humankind to work as
one team. I'd like poverty and hunger to be but a dream. But I
don't like to be disappointed. And after all, those are very big
things. And I'd not like to change myself. I'm just not the
introspective type. And I'm also perfect. No, I'd just like to change
you. Because if everyone like me changed someone like you, we
could all be globally perfect too!

                         ROB
So you're perfect, huh?

                         ALINA

But I wouldn't call myself a perfectionist. I don't like words that end in ist. Fascist, racist, sadist. You may be all of those things, I don't know, I don't know you that well. I just know that the way you ordered your latte a moment ago tells me you think very little of me. That you've dehumanized me.

ROB

(Pointing at the tip jar)
I put my change in the thing ..

ALINA

You put your change in "the thing"?   Am I a vending maching?

ROB

You're a barista, no?

ALINA

But am I not human? If you cut me, would I not bleed espresso? No, I wouldn't. I'd bleed real blood. Duh. So when you order your double cap whip frappe –

ROB

Latte ..

ALINA

… the least you can do is start by looking me in the eyes and say "Hi, how are you?"
(Beat)
To which I would reply: "Good, thanks, and you?"   And you'd say
…
(Gestures to him, "your turn." He looks a little lost)

ROB

Good?

ALINA

Now you've got it!
(Reaches out and shakes his hand, they're still shaking …)
What's your name?

ROB

Rob.

ALINA

Hi Rob. I'm Alina!
          (Finally stops shaking his hand)
What'll you have today?

ROB

A latte. I'll have a latte.
          (Beat)
And maybe a talk with your manager.

ALINA

You want to talk with my manager?

ROB

See, that's the dark side of getting "human" with someone. They
get to know you, they learn your name. They form an opinion.
And the next thing you know, they're using your name against you.
What if I said I plan to report you to the management here for
taking over 10 minutes to make a latte?

ALINA

Well, I'd say that I plan to report you to the High Commissioner for
Human Rights at the U.N. for crimes against humanity.
          (Beat)
But I'll call your bluff. Let me get the manager.
          (She starts walking away)

ROB

No, that's not - I was just kidding-

ALINA

          (She quickly turns back, and addresses him)
Hello, sir, I'm the manager here.

ROB

For real?

                              ALINA
Yep. But today's my last day.
        (Beat)
I'm actually going to work on Wall Street as a portfolio manager.

                              ROB
Oh, don't do that.

                              ALINA
Why not?

                              ROB
Something tells me you wouldn't like all us Wall Street types.
You'd constantly be trying to um … humanize us.

                              ALINA
You deserve to be more than just a stock trading machine don't
you?

                              ROB
Do I?   You'd hate my world.

                              ALINA
I figure the first step in changing your world is climbing to the top
of it. Here's your latte.

                              ROB
She'd written her number on the cup.

                              ALINA
Lust not like.   My taste in men is like my taste in food. I eat junk I
know is horrible for me.   This guy was just more empty calories.

                              ROB
So I called her. I took her to Pe Se, La Bernardin, Momofuko.

                              ALINA

Oh ... the caviar egg with potatoe chips!

ROB

That's some expensive junk food.

ALINA

I'll grant him this, the sex was amazing.

ROB

Her distaste for me aligned beautifully with my own self-loathing.

ALINA

It was like break-up sex. Revenge sex. Hate sex. Just so angry.
Like scratching chicken pox. Feels awesome for a second, then you
realize what you've done to yourself.

ROB

Please, you were super into me.

ALINA

I was into who you could be.

ROB

I was always a numbers guy ... but I started on the sciences side.
An engineer by training in the field of robotics .. I came out of
school wanting to start my own company ...

ALINA

His father gave him one chance to pitch his business idea ... if his
Dad thought it had legs, he'd fund it ... if not ...

ROB

I agreed that if not ... I'd give trading a try. Dad felt my math skills
were better applied in finance than in science.

ALINA

Money, money, money.

ROB

I had a dream of engineering lifelike, artificially intelligent robotic puppies for allergic children.

                    ALINA
His dad thought it was a non-starter.

                    ROB
I told him, I said "Dad, do you know how many kids are allergic to dogs? The market is huge!" And he said:

                    ALINA
"The market is in your head."

                    ROB
Every kid deserves to have a dog!

                    ALINA
Robert didn't have a dog as a kid.

                    ROB
Dad told me I was allergic.

                    ALINA
But you weren't!

                    ROB
Dad said if he got me a dog, my throat would close up and I'd die.

                    ALINA
He just didn't want a dog around the house!

                    ROB
Despite his doubts, dad gave me a chance to pitch out. I stood in front of him and a panel of his VC cronies. Demoed my prototype robo-pup with my allergic neice.
        (Pulls a little stuffed puppy out from behind somewhere)
Ruff-ruff. Ruff-ruff …

                    ALINA

(Little girl voice)
No please I'm allergic! I'll die.

ROB
(Coming closer)
Ruff-ruff.

ALINA
Oh, no … !!!!

ROB
(Puppy pounces)
Ruff-ruff!

ALINA
(Squeeling, he continues going ruff-ruff and having stuffed
pup nuzzle her)
Oooohhh! Oh I love you! I love you little doggie! And I'm not
dead!

ROB
After the demo, their first question was:

ALINA
(Old man voice)
"Do these robotic puppies have a military application?"

ROB
They wanted me to weaponize my robotic puppies!
(Beat)
I tried drawing rocket launchers on the backs of my puppies … but
my heart wasn't in it.
(Beat)
So a promise is a promise. I gave trading a try. I was … good at it
… very good. Dad was … impressed.

ALINA
Look at you when you say that. "Dad was impressed." Your whole
face lights up.

ROB

No it doesn't.

ALINA

You know, if we had tied the knot … you would have had to swear vows, you know? A husband has to put his wife above all others … even his parents. Even your father. But to you, your father - who golfs with Warren Buffett – he is everything to you.
(Beat)
You've put him above yourself even.   You're scared to be who you really are.

ROB

Who I really am is a damn fine trader.
(Beat)
Not unlike yourself.

ALINA

Under Rob's tutelage … I was learning to trade.

ROB

And getting damn good at it.

ALINA

However, I wouldn't trade just any stocks …

ROB

"Ethical investing" is slowing you down.

ALINA

You mean slowing *you* down.

ROB

Socially screened funds are a fraction of the market Alina!
(Beat)
I had an incredible opportunity to handle trades for some of my father's influential friends.

ALINA

The New Year's Eve party …

ROB

She'd pulled me away at a very important moment. I needed to get back down there …

ALINA

His father has this beautiful skydeck on the third floor of their home … I wanted a moment for us … just for us.

(Music plays, lights change to indicate the stars around them, they both have champagne glasses in hand)

ALINA

Here's how it goes.

5, 4, 3, 2, 1 - Happy New Year!

You take my face gently in your hands, pull my lips to yours. Then bringing your arms down around me, your hands come to rest softly but firmly on my shoulder blades. You pull me into you. Close.

I breathe in. My nose buried in your neck. I breathe out. Ahhhh. In your arms. I let it all go. Everything I've been carrying, I let it go. My shoulders drop. My neck relaxes. I'm safe. I'm ready to begin again. With you.

That's how it goes, Robbie. And it's less than one minute to midnight. But that's how it goes. If you stay here.

Downstairs, they're all having fun. They won't miss us. Their champagne will flow without us. Afterwards, their year ahead will march on without us. And we'll be … together. Just you and I. Because you cared enough to be here with me. Really here with me.

Down there with them I can't feel your touch.   Your father said if you want to run with the big dogs, you have to get off the porch. But if you want to run with them … you're going to leave me behind.

It's up to you. Please. Only a few seconds left. What will the new year bring?

5, 4, 3, 2 …. 1.

(Music fades. They put their glasses down.)

ROB

I had to go back down.

ALINA

I wanted you to stay with me.

ROB

So you could grill me on the silly ideas I had in college.

ALINA

You had inventions … good ideas. Useful ideas. Robotic puppies for allergic children!

ROB

My father never saw the value in puppies..

ALINA

I stood there alone for nearly 15 minutes. I waited as the new year came. I was alone.

ROB

Just for a few minutes.

ALINA

I was alone, but we stayed together.

ROB

A year passed.

ALINA

He continued to invest brilliantly. I continued to invest morally.

ROB

She missed big opportunities.

ALINA

He just saw the money ... the high score.

ROB

She would always talk about what the money could do.

ALINA

The foundation of every great relationship is a Foundation.

ROB

She wanted to start a foundation.

ALINA

He wasn't into it. That's when the nightmares began.

ROB

She had this recurring one where I guess I was a teenager ...

ALINA

It's the one with you as the poster child for the entire human race.
        (Beat)
If the poster-child were a spoiled adolescent.
        (Beat)
I'm in an Oz-like place. Dressed like Dorothy. I approach a green castle, but not made of Emeralds, made of money. I knock on the door. The doorman greets me.

ROB

        (British accent)
Who goes there? You here to see All of Humanity?

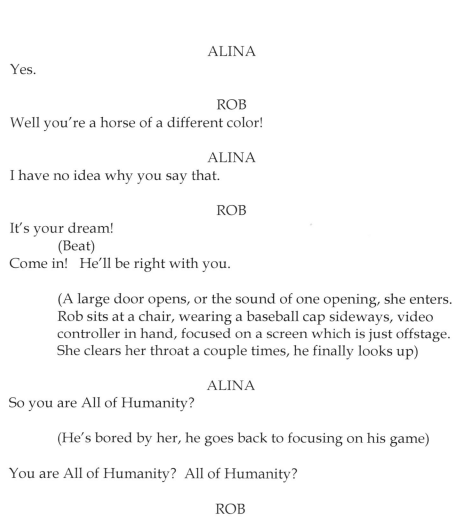

ALINA

Yes.

ROB

Well you're a horse of a different color!

ALINA

I have no idea why you say that.

ROB

It's your dream!
        (Beat)
Come in!   He'll be right with you.

        (A large door opens, or the sound of one opening, she enters.
        Rob sits at a chair, wearing a baseball cap sideways, video
        controller in hand, focused on a screen which is just offstage.
        She clears her throat a couple times, he finally looks up)

ALINA

So you are All of Humanity?

        (He's bored by her, he goes back to focusing on his game)

You are All of Humanity?   All of Humanity?

ROB

Yep ...

ALINA

You are not what I expected you'd look like.

ROB

        (Still looking at his game)
What'd you expect?

ALINA

Well ... not ... You look kinda like my 14 year old nephew.

ROB

Cool, cool.

ALINA

I'm told I only have two minutes with you. To talk some sense into you. And I appreciate your time. I'm told the opportunity to address you comes but once in a lifetime ... No pressure, haha. It's just ... ok, you may not like this ... WHAT ARE YOU DOING!?!? Really! Seriously! You are incredibly bright and capable. You put a man on the Moon, created an International Space Station, flew a Rover to Mars! You are on your way to growing up, becoming independent! But you seem distracted to me.

ROB
(Gesturing toward his game)
Distracted? I'm in the zone! I just took this ore-collecting shadow priest to the cleaners! What a sucker! He dropped all his ore to the lowest bidder, ME! Ha.

ALINA

My nephew, he's the same, always distracted. Always playing video games instead of doing his homework. Obsessed with earning "Virtual Gold" on World of Warcraft.

ROB

Piece of advice for him, beware of greedy herb collectors and scribes – always buy your herbs and inks low, sell high – and diversify! Oh, look at the price of that Briarthorne!!!! That's a STEAL!

ALINA

You've created these intricate games where you strive to achieve the highest numeric score. Like my nephew, earning the highest possible numbers drives you. Yet the real numbers, the ones that will advance your sciences so you can move out of your "parents' house" aka the earth ... those numbers you barely look at. Don't you want to be able to live on your own someday? Get your own little place out in the cosmos? That's how you're going to survive long term, right? You're certainly smart enough to do it. But you're distracted.

ROB
Well, if I'm distracted, it's that Orc Shaman's fault! He's driving up prices!!!!! Let's see how he fares against my Bloodlust Uber Spell!!!!

ALINA
And you sure are angry a lot. Like my nephew, he's always fighting with his sister, or anticipating a fight with her, or coming up with great ways to one-up her. He loves drama, he loves conflict.

ROB
YOU ORC-LOVING BASTARD! Sorry, not you- this douchey Mage blocked my spell.

(Over the course of the next bit, Alina moves between him and his screen)

ALINA
You frustrate me, humanity. Because you have all the knowledge to take care of yourself, but you don't apply it. Sure, you have small areas, tiny pockets of health, vitality. But overall, just look at you! The vast majority of you is underfed, malnourished, physically unfit, under-educated. Why don't you focus on improving those numbers?

ROB
I don't know ... it's hard to get organized? Look, you're blocking my view of the game ...

ALINA

Look. Right now, your parents' house is well stocked and you can use the resources here to mature. To study and learn those real numbers and make something of yourself. There's enough so you can nourish all of yourself but …

> (His cell phone rings, he holds a hand up for her to wait a sec while he answers)

ROB

> (Into the phone)

Hey baby!

> (She grabs his phone away)

Yo!

ALINA

…but not if you keep multiplying like you've been - please keep those hormones in check. Like I tell my nephew, there will be plenty of time for dating when you go off to college.

> (Sound of beeping starts)

Oh no. I hear my snooze alarm going off. I guess this is it, my two minutes is up. I hope this is all sinking in because … I'm going to wake up in a second.

ROB

Can I have my phone back?

ALINA

Bottom line, you may not have the time you think you have. A rock could fall out of the sky. You could catch a bad cold. Or have really bad weather … bad things can happen. Use every moment. No more distractions, cut out the fighting and the games. Get serious. Pull yourself together. Focus. Prepare to move out of your parents' house.

> (Beat)

Grow up, Humanity. Please. Grow up.

> (Rob takes off the hat, lights change).

ROB

And then she'd wake up and be mad at me.

ALINA

And for good reason!

ROB

I didn't want to start a Foundation. Or go back to childish pipe-dreams …

ALINA

So instead we went deeper into investing. We became professional angel investors.

ROB

She focused on funding green energy projects.

ALINA

He focused on any business which would earn him more green.

ROB

Another year passed. I started thinking about marriage.

ALINA

His father began to question me everytime I opted to eat the veggies at dinner and skip the meat.

ROB

Green is for one's wallet, not one's plate.

ALINA

You sound just like him.

ROB

So when Thanksgiving came around … things got a little …
        (Scene shifts to a kitchen, he's standing on the other side of a
        door in the dining room)
How's it coming, honey?

ALINA

Fine, everything's fine.

ROB

Are you sure?

ALINA

I'll be out in a minute.

ROB

Is the turkey ready?

ALINA

No, in a minute.

ROB
(He opens the door, pops his head in, voice low)
You said that five minutes ago! Seems like you're hiding in here.
Why are you hiding in here?

ALINA
Fine, come in. Close the door.   You want to know why I'm
"hiding" in here?
Because out there your mother's all "Happy Turkey Day, Alina!"
and "We're so pleased you decided to host this year" and "You're
making such a lovely home for our son" and finally "Oh, doesn't
she look pretty in that dress I bought her, dear?" to which your
father replies…

ROB
"Mmm-hmm, sweeter than pumpkin pie."

(They both laugh at his impression)

ALINA

I wanted to reply "I'm so glad that despite the eight mergers I helped broker between sustainable energy companies for work, it's the smell of turkey in the oven and the way I wear a Laura Ashley dress that proves I'm worth my salt."

                              ROB
Thank you for not doing that.

                              ALINA
You're welcome. No, Instead I say "Thanks – let me check on the turkey."   And that brings us here.
          (Beat)
Did you know your mother called me last month?   Asked me to do this for you.   Said you complained about last year's Thanksgiving to her.   Said you didn't have the heart to tell me that eating Tofurky with my girlfriends while watching back-to-back screenings of *Dances with Wolves* and *Last of the Mohicans* wasn't really your thing.

                              ROB
I'm sorry she did that … I'll talk to her.

                              ALINA
Talk to *me*, Rob! I had no idea you felt this way. I thought you liked my anti-establishment Thanksgiving "thing" as much as I did. I thought you agreed that the genocide and subjugation of an indigenous people by a stronger invading culture was not cause for annual celebration.   And maybe your mother had just heard what she wanted to hear, or taken something you'd said out of context.

So I went to you and I asked "What would you think about having a more traditional Thanksgiving this year with your parents?" To which you replied:

                              ROB
"Sure, that'd be nice."

                              ALINA

"Sure, that'd be nice." I thought you'd say "But honey, aren't you opposed to cooking and eating animals when there are perfectly good plant foods we can enjoy?" But no, you were strangely uninquisitive, just …

                          ROB
"Sure, that'd be nice."

                         ALINA
Like my sudden transformation from animal rights advocate into Stepford Wife turkey killer was perfectly normal. And maybe I should have just freaked out at that point and let you know how upset I was.

                          ROB
Maybe.

                         ALINA
I don't know, I was in shock. So I just said "Well, but maybe not. We don't want to be like the rest of America, contributing to the November Turkey Genocide." I joked "We couldn't live with the guilt." And you said:

                          ROB
"Well, it's only one month out of the year, and besides the president pardons a turkey to make up for it."

                         ALINA
Or *does* he? I decided to learn about the pardoned turkey's happy retirement to soothe myself.

In the process I uncovered urban legend keepers who tell of a wealthy "benefactor" who donates millions each year to the farm where the pardoned turkey goes. In exchange, the pardoned turkey is transferred to his estate. And then, according to black-market-turkey.com, the benefactor eats our national symbol for mercy and kindness.

So most likely, the story of the pardoned turkey is a fairy tale we sell the masses to alleviate their collective guilt, when in actuality some rich bastard is stealing that turkey's retirement every year!

ROB

C'mon Alina. That's crazy conspiracy theory stuff. I'm sure the pardoned turkey enjoys his retirement.

ALINA

And what if he does? That's still just ONE turkey. What about all the other millions of turkeys? Do they get pardoned too?
    (Pointing to the turkey she's cooked)
Did Mr. Butterball right there get pardoned? Did I?
    (Beat)
All this month, I kept hoping any moment you'd grant me a reprieve, let me off the hook. Tell me it wasn't right for me to make this sacrifice. That it was okay if I wanted to spend the holiday in a sweat lodge saying penance. But instead you stood idly by as I cooked away my identity so your family could have "a nice dinner."
    (Beat)
You've got me trading way more than stocks, Rob.

ROB

So what do you want me to do? Should I send them home? Cancel Thanksgiving?

ALINA

No. No, because Mr. Butterball there has already made his sacrifice and so have I. Because there really are no pardons for turkeys tonight. Because I'm a real turkey for going along with all of this. And because you're a real turkey for letting me.
    (Beat)
Now go back out there, please. I told you. I need a minute.

ROB

So I went back out to my parents in the dining room, and a moment later she came out with Mr. Butterball. Smiling, like our kitchen encounter had never happened.

ALINA

I gave him and his family the night they wanted. He never actually said "I'm sorry."

ROB

A month passed and she never mentioned it again. Like she wasn't mad at all.

ALINA

Why get mad? I prefer to get *even*.

ROB

Later that year, at the Christmas party of the company owned by my dad's wealthiest buddy ... she was invited to speak. She's a great speaker, but no one saw this one coming ...

    (She's at a podium)

ALINA

I look out at a sea of men in suits. A few token women scattered throughout ... and it just came to me.
    (Beat)
World peace, world peace. Everyone wants world peace. Or everyone pretends to want world peace. But they don't really want world peace. Because there's a simple way to get it. Everyone knows it, no one wants to say it. Fire the boys. Fire the boys! There. I said it.

The boys have been mostly in charge of the world for a long time now, and look at it. The world is a mess. A mess created by boys. And why are we surprised by this? Go into any single boy's home or apartment or dorm room. Go into it. Is it tidy? Are the pants crisply folded, the shirts carefully hung, the socks darned? Some? Sure, sure. Some are. But the majority? The majority are a forgotten wasteland of dirty laundry, empty beer cans and old pizza boxes! So what idiot saw the average boy's room and said, "This looks good! We should put this guy in charge of the entire world! I think he'll get the place in order!" I can tell you this, it wasn't a girl. A girl did not make that decision.

No, boys have been putting other boys in charge for a long time now. And yeah, we girls get some middle management positions, a few leadership roles here and there. Things are changing. But meanwhile, the boys really are still mainly in charge. And really, if they knew what is good for them, they'd all step down and let some ladies step up right away.

And I know, boys, what you're thinking "What makes you think you'd do better!" And my answer is, wild baboons! Wild baboons have proved that girls can do better. Let me explain.

There's a troupe of wild baboons in Africa, you can Google this, where a tragedy killed off most of the males, leaving all the girl monkeys in charge. And the result was AMAZE-BALLS. The baboons stopped fighting amongst themselves, and spent more time socializing and grooming each other. Making them less mean and more clean!

And it was good for the boys! The boy monkeys who used to be all stressed out, worrying about competing with the other boys , learned from the now dominant girl culture how to groom each other. In no other baboon troupe does one male monkey groom another. These secure guy monkeys do! The girls taught them that! And when new boys come into the troupe, they teach them how to do it too. And they've kept this monkey utopia going for generation after generation! And the result is healthier boy monkeys!

The scientist who studies them – Dr. Sapolsky – found these monkeys have none of the stress-related issues of regular monkeys. Regular monkeys, especially the lower status ones that get picked on all the time, have the same problems we do - high blood pressure, obesity, and impaired brain function from stress. But Sapolksy's monkeys don't, no – they're thriving like no other troupe.

So boys, if you know what's good for you – you will step down right now and let the girls take over. Not only will it be good for your individual health, it will be good for the entire world!

ROB

It wasn't good for business. A lot of people didn't want to work with us after that …

ALINA

A lot of the woman came up to me and shook my hand after that.
(Beat)
After that, he was a little cold, distant.

ROB

I was embarrassed.

ALINA

We stopped talking about our future. I couldn't see a future in a relationship where the real me … the real you, Rob … didn't have a place.
(Beat)
So I said goodbye. I've said goodbye.

ROB

And I'm still trying to find a way to get her to say hello again.

ALINA

I invest on my own now. Promising inventors of new technologies and social causes. Lately, I've been looking at how other countries handle their prison systems. Unlike us, with our 80% return to prison rate ... some countries have got it down to only 20%. What the hell are we doing wrong?

ROB
She won't return my calls. So I read her column in the Huffington Post.

ALINA
After my little speech, Arianna and I became fast friends. In my column, I talk about the work I've been doing with prison psychologists and researchers of the prisons here in our country, interested in new methods of rehabilitation.

ROB
Love is the mother of invention.

ALINA
Today, I've got an inventor who sounds very interesting. He's mysterious though, calls himself John Doe.

ROB
Of course it's me.

ALINA
I see ... I get up to go. Wasting my time ...

ROB
I'm not here to waste your time, Alina!

ALINA
You're an investor, not an inventor!

ROB
I haven't invested in months. I couldn't tell you if the Dow is up or down. I can only tell you I've been down ... ever since ... well, you know.

(Beat)

I have a real proposal for you. I promise.

ALINA

We'll see. Go ahead.

ROB

So here goes. I'm going to give my pitch. It's Alina and a room full of prison psychologists … I have butterflies.
　　　(Beat)
Here goes.
　　　(Beat)
Ladies and gentleman.
　　　(Clears through, beat)
You study the behavior of convicted murderers, right? How many of them tell you that they were cuddling with an adorable puppy when they snapped? None, right?

So why don't we lock them away with puppies? Yes, there might be a risk they would kill the puppies. But what if those puppies couldn't be killed? What if I told you I had a way to engineer a puppy for both optimal cuteness and indestructibility?

I know, it sounds like sci-fi, but it's not. In Japan, they already have adorable white robotic seals that bring joy to the elderly and infirm. Look it up, Google robotic seals Japan!

What if we could engineer a totally lifelike, indestructible super puppy? I tell you it can be done, and you won't know the difference between it and a standard puppy, except if you try to snap its neck its impossible.

Now, we take a room full of those puppies and we put the most hardened gang banger in there. At first they may try to kill the puppies. Sure, we'd expect that. That's why it's so important these puppies are indestructible.

Soon, the murderer, exhausted from the futility of trying to snap unbreakable puppy neck, falls into a state of learned helplessness. They begin to cry in despair "Why, why can't I kill these puppies! Why!?"

At that moment they are vulnerable and our super-puppies close in, licking and nuzzling and staring with their perfectly round adorable eyes. Their little puppy paws will be perfectly designed to hit ticklish spots and what is going to happen is those criminals will begin to giggle. And all the while these puppies will just keep coming and coming and coming at them with their relentless cuteness. And these puppies never get tired.

Imagine it, someone who has grown up in a violent landscape filled with conflict and abuse. Instead of putting them into a locked environment filled with more of that, what if we said "Put him in the Puppy Room!"

At first they might say "No, please, no, no … not the Puppy Room!" Because what self respecting hardened man or woman wants to commune with puppies? Cuteness is the enemy of toughness. But faced with this unbearable cuteness and incredible unflappable affection, their anger, their fear, their hate will be overwhelmed by love.

Yes, I have a dream of invincible super-puppies. They will not just be cute and unkillable, a marvel of modern engineering, but they will lift humanity out of the darkness.

Now … Who among you is going to fund my research?!

       (ALINA raises her hand, ROB smiles. Fade to black).

FIN

Copyright © 2016 by Gabriel Davis

ISBN-13: 978-1535215947
ISBN-10: 1535215941

Printed in Great
Britain
by Amazon